He was visiting his cousins during the Dussehra holidays. His Pishi (Aunt) and didi were waiting to meet him.

Pronunciation tip to parent:
V is pronounced by biting the lower lip.
W is pronounced by making an O with the lips. Many 'W' words have been used in the book to provide practice.

Welcome!

The next day, Pishi and Didi took them to see the wonderful Victoria Memorial.

It celebrates its 100th year in 2021 and was built during the British Raj as a tribute to Queen Victoria.
Wow!

They took a 'tonga' ride. Shivi had never been in a horse carriage before. He loved the wind in his hair and the clippity-cloppity sounds.

They passed the Eden Garden Stadium.
Didi exclaimed with pride,
"It's the oldest cricket stadium in India
and the third largest in the world!"

In the evening, they went pandal hopping to worship Durga Maa.

Durga Puja celebrates the victory of good over evil.
Maa makes all your wishes come true!
Which traditional festival is celebrated in your city?

On the third day, they sat in the Metro. Kolkata Metro is the first metro in India.

CALCUT

I'm going to become a paleontologist when I grow up!
HEATRE

They went to the Science City.
Shivi loved the dinosaurs.

From there, they went to the Alipore Zoo.
Do you think animals like it when they are put in cages?
ALIPORE ZOO
The Royal Bengal Tiger is the national animal of India!

THE ROYAL BENGAL TIGER
Or maybe I'll become a vet.

Shivi then saw a train running in the middle of the city. He was confused.

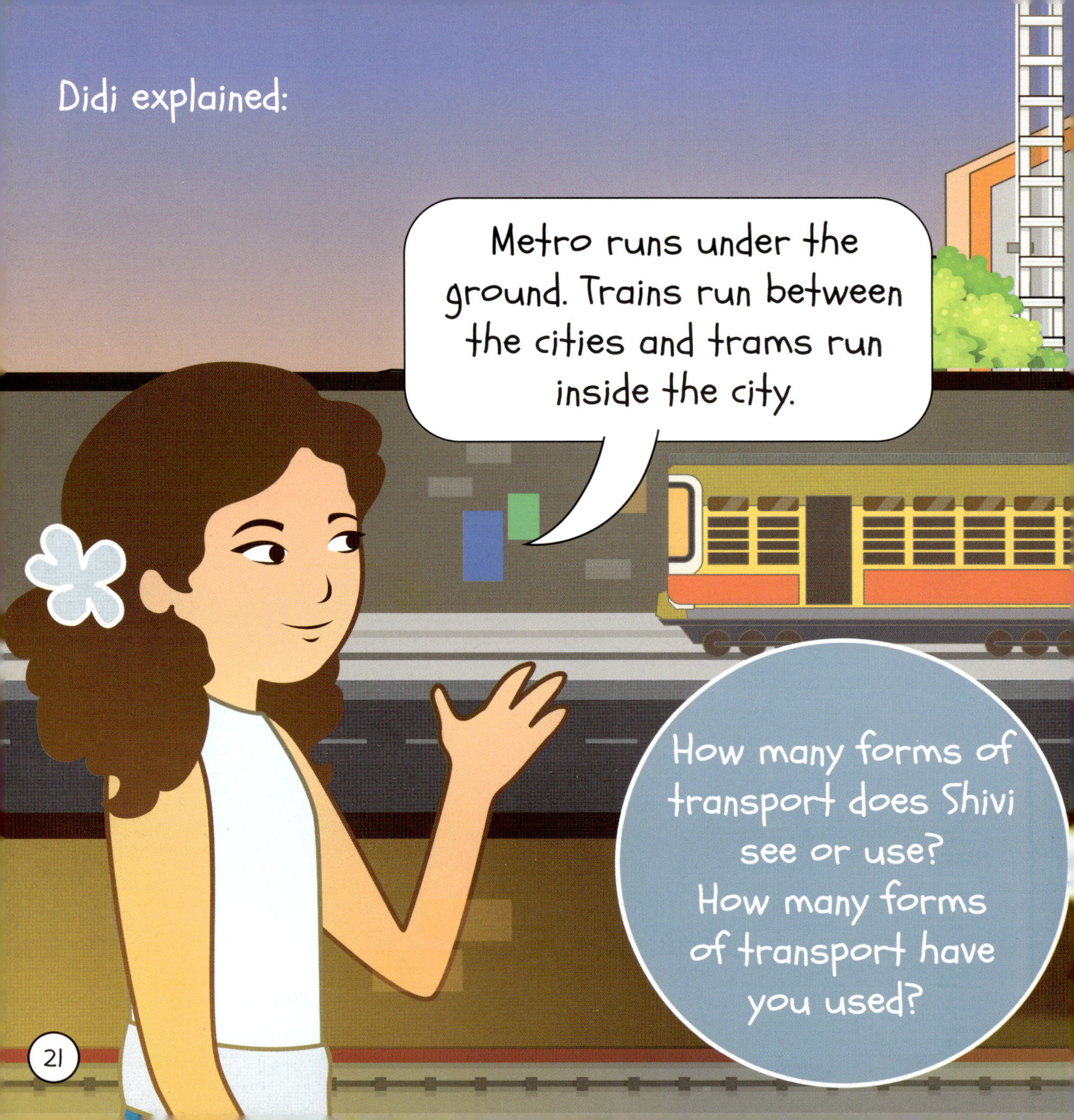
Didi explained:
Metro runs under the ground. Trains run between the cities and trams run inside the city.
How many forms of transport does Shivi see or use? How many forms of transport have you used?

Train
Tram
Metro

On the way back, they stopped fo
Kolkata's famous street food.
They enjoyed the 'muri, puchka
and rosogolla'.

Rosogolla is a sweet made from milk. Muri and puchka—if you don't know, then you must visit Kolkata soon to experience it!

Out of the window of his cab, Shivi saw a weak boy. He was whistling, but he looked hungry.

Some children don't get food. You should be glad you do.

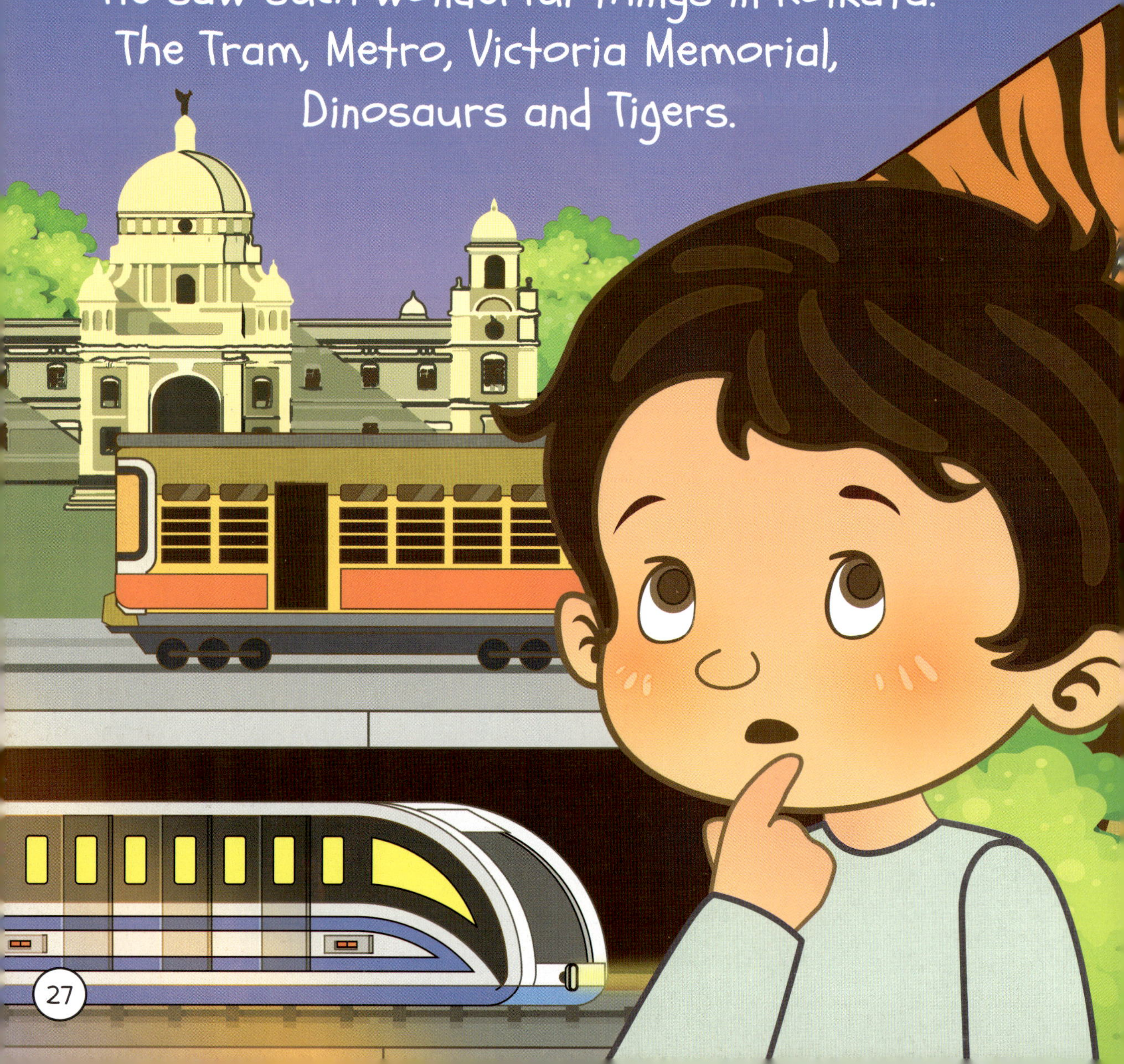

He saw such wonderful things in Kolkata.
The Tram, Metro, Victoria Memorial,
Dinosaurs and Tigers.

But he also remembered the little boy's eyes. And he remembered Didi's words, "Some children don't get food. You should be glad you do."

After he got home, Shivi washed himself and had wate
He decided never to waste food again.

When he woke up in the morning, Pishi was singing wonderful Rabindra Sangeet.

Rabindra Sangeet was composed by the Nobel Laureate, Rabindra Nath Tagore and is sacred to every Bengali household.
ipode more
kkha koro...

In Bengal, "aaschi" is said as a goodbye instead of "bye", which means "I will visit again".

It was the last day of his holiday! Shivi loved Kolkata and wants to visit it again during his next holiday. So he didn't say 'Bye', he said 'Aashchi'.

# Bipade More Rokkha Karo

Bipade more rokkha karo e nohe mor praartharna – Bipade aami naa jeno kori bhoy.
It is not my prayer that you save me from all perils I pray that I should not fear when faced with odds

Dukkhotaape byathito chite naai baa dile santanaa, Dukkhey jeno korite paari joy.
Console me not when I am torn with misery Grant me instead the will to win agains grief

Sahaay mor naa jodi jute nijer bol naa jeno tute – Songsaarete ghotile khoti, lobhile shudhu banchona, Nijer mone naa jeno maani khoy.

If no help comes forth, let my strength not crumble When losses abound and I am deprived of everything Let my heart not take this as defeat

Aamare tumi koribe traan e nahe mor praarthana – Torite paari shakoti jeno roy.

Protect me from the storms is not my prayer Bless me the strength to sail througl

Aamar bhaar laaghab kori naai baa dile santana, Bohite paari emoni jeno hoy.

Need you not comfort me by lightening my burden Bless me instead with the fortituc to bear

Namroshire sukhero dine tomari mukh loibo chine – Dukher raate nikhilo dhara je di kare banchona
Tomare jeno na kori sangshoy.

I know your presence when I bow to you in my days of prosperity In my darkest nights when the whole world turns against me Let me not ever doubt You.



Source - geetabitan.co

## What do you enjoy most on your trips?

Date: